GETTING TO KNOW THE WORLD'S GREATEST ARTISTS

REMBRANDT

WRITTEN AND ILLUSTRATED BY MIKE VENEZIA

CHILDRENS PRESS ®

CHICAGO

Cover: *The Night Watch*. 1642. Canvas, 359 x 438 cm. Amsterdam, Rijksmuseum

Dedicated to Jeannine, Mike, and Liz

The author wishes to express a special thanks to Sarah Mollman

Library of Congress Cataloging-in-Publication Data

Venezia, Mike.
    Rembrandt / written and illustrated by Mike Venezia.
        p.   cm. — (Getting to know the world's greatest artists)
    Summary: Briefly examines the life and work of the
seventeenth-century Dutchman who was one of the greatest
artists of all time.
    ISBN 0-516-02272-5
    1. Rembrandt Harmenszoon van Rijn. 1606-1669—Juvenile
literature. 2. Painters—Netherlands—Biography—Juvenile
literature. 3. Painting, Dutch—Juvenile
literature. 4. Painting, Modern—17th-18th centuries—
Netherlands—Juvenile literature. [1. Rembrandt
Harmenszoon van Rijn, 1606-1669. 2. Artists. 3. Painting,
Dutch. 4. Painting, Modern—Netherlands. 5. Art
appreciation.] I. Rembrandt Harmenszoon van Rijn, 1606-
1669. II. Title. III. Series.
ND653.R4V498   1988   87-33014
759.9492—dc19   CIP
[92]   AC

Childrens Press®, Chicago
Copyright ©1988 by Regensteiner Publishing Enterprises, Inc.
All rights reserved. Published simultaneously in Canada.
Printed in the United States of America.
        8 9 10 R 97 96

Rembrandt was one of the greatest artists of all time. He lived and painted in Holland. He was born in 1606 and died in 1669.

View of Amsterdam. 1640. Etching, 11.3 x 15.4 cm. Chicago, The Art Institute. Clarence Buckingham Collection

This is the city of Amsterdam in Holland, where Rembrandt spent most of his time painting and drawing.

As you can see, there were lots of windmills back then.

In fact, Rembrandt's father owned
a windmill. Rembrandt probably had
lots of fun when he was growing up.

Even though there were no cameras in Rembrandt's time, we know what he looked like because he was always painting pictures of himself, maybe more than any other famous artist.

Self-Portrait. 1629.
Panel, 37.5 x 29 cm.
The Hague, Mauritshuis.
Scala/Art Resource

This painting was done when Rembrandt was twenty-three years old.

Self-Portrait. 1658. Canvas, 131 x 102 cm. New York, The Frick Collection

This is Rembrandt when he was a little older, and a little heavier.

There seems to be a big change in the way he painted, too.

Rembrandt liked to paint at home and spend lots of time with his family.

In spite of this, he painted over five hundred pictures!

Rembrandt used his family and relatives as models in many of his works.

Rembrandt's Mother. 1631. Panel, 60 x 48 cm. Amsterdam, Rijksmuseum

This is his mother, reading the Bible.

Bearded Man in Furred Oriental Cape and Robe. 1631. Etching, Half length, 14.5 x 12.9 cm.
Chicago, The Art Institute. Clarence Buckingham Collection

This is his father, wearing a furry
cape and hat. Rembrandt also used
his sister and wife as models.

Titus at a Desk. 1655. Canvas, 77 x 63 cm. Rotterdam, Museum Boymans-van Beuningen

This is Rembrandt's son, Titus, doing homework. He looks as if he's stuck on a math problem or daydreaming, just like kids do today.

The Feast of Belshazzar. Canvas, 167 x 209.5 cm. London, The National Gallery

Rembrandt is well known for his use of light and dark paints. The darkness in his paintings helps to make the light parts stand out.

The people in this painting were pretty messy, by the way. As you can

see, at least two glasses of wine are being knocked over at the same time!

Sometimes Rembrandt would paint very smoothly, and sometimes he would pile on the paint. In *The Feast of Belshazzar*, he did both.

Detail of *The Feast of Belshazzar* on page 12

As you can see, the people and things around them are pretty smooth looking.

The gold and jewels Belshazzar is wearing are loaded with thick paint. This makes them look like they're glowing and they seem almost real!

An Artist in His Studio. Panel, 25 x 32 cm. Boston, Museum of Fine Arts. Zoe Oliver Sherman Collection

It's not clear whether this is a self-portrait or a painting of one of Rembrandt's students or friends. In any case, we can get an idea of what an artist's studio looked like in the 1600s.

Portrait of a Lady. Canvas, 11.8 x 88.9 cm.
New York, The Metropolitan Museum of Art. H.O. Havemeyer Collection

Because there weren't any cameras in Rembrandt's time, many people wanted their pictures painted.

Most of the people Rembrandt painted wore black clothes and wanted to look very serious. It was the style of the day.

Rembrandt and Saskia. Canvas, 161 x 131 cm.
Dresden, Staatliches Kunstasammlungen. Giraudon/Art Resource

So, for fun, Rembrandt would dress up in bright clothes and jewels and then paint himself.

This is a picture of Rembrandt and his wife, Saskia. Rembrandt looks like he is having a good time.

Self-Portrait in Oriental Costume. 1631. Panel, 81 x 54 cm. Paris, Petit Palais

Here he is *really* dressed up, with his pet dog. Rembrandt liked dogs and you can see them in many of his paintings.

This is probably Rembrandt's greatest portrait. It's a painting of a group of important men. Their job was to make sure all the cloth made in Amsterdam was made just right.

Rembrandt painted the group of men looking right at *you*. It's almost like you walked in during their meeting and they stopped to see what you wanted. They seem friendly and concerned.

Few painters have ever made a portrait look so natural and real.

The Syndics of the Drapers' Guild. 1662. Canvas, 185 x 274 cm. Amsterdam, Rijksmuseum. Scala/Art Resource

Rembrandt painted many scenes from the Bible. The only thing was he dressed people in whatever costumes he liked, and used furniture and other things from his own time.

Do you think people from Bible times would recognize themselves?

Tobias Healing His Father's Blindness. 1636. Panel, 48 x 39 cm. Stuttgart, Staatsgalerie

The Night Watch. 1642. Canvas, 359 x 438 cm. Amsterdam, Rijksmuseum

One of Rembrandt's greatest paintings, *The Night Watch,* was the start of a lot of his problems.

A group of soldiers asked Rembrandt if he would paint a portrait of them to hang in their

clubhouse. Rembrandt agreed, but thought he would try something different.

He thought the painting would look more natural and not as stiff as other portraits of the day if he placed everybody standing around talking and getting ready to go for a march. Rembrandt was right, but he made a lot of people angry, especially the people who paid to be in the painting. They all wanted to be the same size.

Rembrandt's wife, Saskia, had been sick for a long time, and while he was painting *The Night Watch*, she died. This made Rembrandt very sad, and when he found out the soldiers were unhappy with his painting, he was even sadder.

He kept on painting anyway, and he decided he didn't care what people thought of his work.

His paintings got even better! It's funny how things like that can happen sometimes.

Hendrickje Stoffels as Venus. 1662. Canvas, 110 x 88 cm. Paris, Louvre

After Saskia died, a lady named Hendrickje moved into Rembrandt's house to take care of Titus. Rembrandt and Hendrickje fell in love and Rembrandt painted many pictures of her. Later they had a baby girl named Cornelia.

The Mill. 1650. Canvas, 87.5 x 105.5 cm. Washington, National Gallery of Art. Widener Collection

Rembrandt is best known for his paintings of people, but he also did paintings in which the scenery is the most important part of the picture. These paintings are called landscapes.

Even though people paid Rembrandt a lot for his paintings, he never seemed to have any money. This was because he bought a big,

expensive house and collected all
kinds of things.

He paid lots of money for other
artists' work, jewelry, antiques,
armor, fancy clothes, gold helmets,
and statues. He used these things in
his paintings.

Rembrandt lived to be sixty-three years old. He painted right up to the end of his life. In fact, when he died, he left an unfinished painting called *Simeon in the Temple.*

Maybe the most important thing about Rembrandt's paintings are his people. If you look at them closely

Detail of *The Syndics of the Drapers' Guild* on page 21

Detail of *Tobias Healing His Father's Blindness* on page 23

Detail of *The Night Watch* on page 24

Details (left and above left) of
Rembrandt with Saskia on page 18

and forget about the funny clothes
they wore, or where Rembrandt
placed them, they almost seem like
people you might know today.

Rembrandt made the people he
painted seem alive, even more real
than a photograph could.

That's why many people think he's
the greatest painter who ever lived.

It's much better to see a real Rembrandt painting than a picture of one. Look for his paintings in your art museum.

The pictures in this book came from the museums listed below. If none of these museums is close to you, maybe you can visit one when you are on vacation.

Rijksmuseum, Amsterdam, The Netherlands
Mauritshuis, The Hague, The Netherlands
The Frick Collection, New York, New York
The Art Institute, Chicago, Illinois
Museum Boymans-van Beuningen, Rotterdam, The Netherlands
The National Gallery, London, England
Museum of Fine Arts, Boston, Massachusetts
The Metropolitan Museum of Art, New York, New York
Staatliches Kunstasammlungen, Dresden, East Germany
Petit Palais, Paris, France
Staatsgalerie, Stuttgart, West Germany
Louvre, Paris, France
National Gallery of Art, Washington, D. C.